You Wake Up One Morning

A Kid's Prompted Journal for Creating
Great Stories in Words and Art.

The Small-Tooth-Dog Publishing Group
Tolleson, Arizona

How to Use this Prompted Journal.

This journal is designed to help express your creativity. Creativity is imagination that is focused.

There is only one rule: This is your journal. Use it the way you want.

Here are a few ideas.

A journal is a place to keep your thoughts, writings, and art. Most people who keep journals make entries in them on a regular basis, such as every day or once per week.

A "prompted journal," is a journal that contains "prompts" or suggestions that might help you write or draw in the journal on a regular basis. This journal has more than 50 prompts.

These prompts are based on the idea that you wake up one morning (ywuom) and discover something unusual about your life, something that was not there or was not happening the night before.

There is a list of these "you wake up one morning" prompts on the next few pages. Read through them all. Maybe circle the ones you first want to write about or illustrate. You don't have to use them all and you don't have to do them in order.

Use your creativity to make the best use of the following pages. The pages with lines might be used to write on. The blank pages or the graphic-novel style pages might be used for art or doodling.

However, you aren't limited to writing on the lined pages. Write or draw on them. Do whatever you like.

On the blank pages, you aren't required to draw or create art. You can write if you like or do what feels right for you.

About being creative.

When you were a little kid, it might have been hard for you think of "abstract" ideas. Now that you are older, you should be able to think "abstractly" about the prompts in this book. Abstract means that you think about a prompt beyond what the words by themselves mean.

For example, the prompt might read,

"YWUOM and someone has built a giant statue of you."

Little kids might draw a statue that is very tall. That is fine to do if you are a little kid.

However, think "abstractly" about that statue of you. Is it the tallest statue in the world? Is it only a tiny bit taller than you? Were you surprised by the statue or did you know that it was being built? What does the statue show you are doing? Do you like the statue? Was the statue made by a friend? Was the person happy or sad when they made your statue? Is there something wrong with the statue? Is it a perfect statue? Does it come to life? Is it missing pieces?

Write or draw something that shows your thinking about the statue.

Repeat this process for each prompt you choose. Think deeply about the many ideas that might come with each prompt.

Have a great time!

You Wake Up One Morning (Ywuom) . . .
Suggestion: Check the ☐ when you have used the prompt.

☐ Ywuom and you have grown three feet (one meter) taller.

☐ Ywuom and you have all the money you could ever want.

☐ Ywuom and your pet can speak to you.

☐ Ywuom and you are the principal of a school.

☐ Ywuom and you can only sing to communicate.

☐ Ywuom and there is a huge party going on downstairs.

☐ Ywuom in a room with nothing in it except two doors. One reads, "Go through this door." The other door reads "No, go through this door instead."

☐ Ywuom and you can understand every language on earth.

☐ Ywuom and you are the president or leader of your country.

☐ Ywuom and you are the most popular entertainer on earth.

☐ Ywuom and you can drive a car.

☐ Ywuom and your house is filled with only your favorite food.

☐ Ywuom morning and you are a fish in the ocean.

☐ Ywuom and you have a private airplane to take you anywhere you want at any time you want to go.

☐ Ywuom and it is 200 years into the future. However, you are still the same age as you are now.

☐ Ywuom and there are no computers, smart phones or internet anywhere in the world.

☐ Ywuom and you are 20 years older than you are now.

☐ Ywuom and you can have breakfast with anyone you want who was or is alive.

☐ Ywuom and you have invented (coded) the most important computer program ever made.

☐ Ywuom and you are the greatest chef or cook in the world.

You Wake Up One Morning (Ywuom) . . .

- ☐ Ywuom and you are living in ancient Egypt.

- ☐ Ywuom and you are living in the American Old West.

- ☐ Ywuom and cats are now in charge of the world.

- ☐ Ywuom and you are living in a colony on the moon.

- ☐ Ywuom and everyone has forgotten who you are.

- ☐ Ywuom and you are the greatest sports star in the world.

- ☐ Ywuom and you are a character in a video game.

- ☐ Ywuom and you own a giant amusement park.

- ☐ Ywuom and everyone around you always has really bad breath.

- ☐ Ywuom and you can be invisible all day.

- ☐ Ywuom and you are the strongest person in the world.

- ☐ Ywuom and you are only six inches (150mm) tall.

- ☐ Ywuom and you can read the minds of everyone else.

- ☐ Ywuom and you have three wishes.

- ☐ Ywuom and you can grant only one wish of anyone you know.

- ☐ Ywuom and aliens from another planet have come to your city.

- ☐ Ywuom and you have a robot that can do whatever you command.

- ☐ Ywuom and you can fly.

- ☐ Ywuom and you will never be afraid again.

- ☐ Ywuom and you are in a spaceship traveling to another galaxy.

- ☐ Ywuom and someone has made a giant statue of you.

You Wake Up One Morning (Ywuom) . . .

- [ ] Ywuom and you are a world-famous author.

- [ ] Ywuom and you can't stop laughing.

- [ ] Ywuom and you never have to sleep again.

- [ ] Ywuom and you learn the weather will be perfect for you forever.

- [ ] Ywuom and you have the world's largest feet.

- [ ] Ywuom and you can make any plant grow at any time.

- [ ] Ywuom in the dark and it will never be light again.

- [ ] Ywuom and you can play every instrument in the world.

- [ ] Ywuom and you are the smartest person in the world.

- [ ] Ywoum and your skin, hair, and eyes are colored purple.

- [ ] Ywuom and you can see the sky through a brand-new hole in your ceiling.

- [ ] Ywuom and you have magic shoes that can take you anywhere.

- [ ] Ywuom and there is a tiger sleeping in your room.

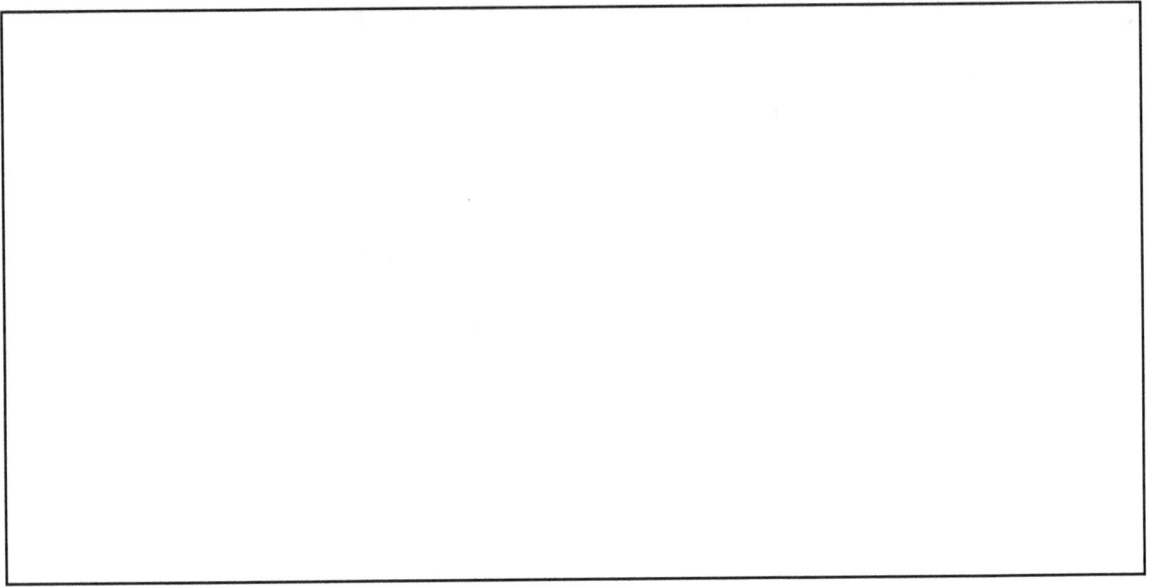